Cambridge Discovery Education™
▶ INTERACTIVE READERS

Series editor: Bob Hastings

TRAPPED!
THE ARON RALSTON STORY

B2+

Caroline Shackleton and Nathan Paul Turner

CAMBRIDGE
UNIVERSITY PRESS

DISCOVERY
EDUCATION™

CAMBRIDGE
UNIVERSITY PRESS

32 Avenue of the Americas, New York, NY 10013-2473, USA

Cambridge University Press is part of the University of Cambridge.

It furthers the University's mission by disseminating knowledge in the pursuit of education, learning and research at the highest international levels of excellence.

www.cambridge.org
Information on this title: www.cambridge.org/9781107669987

© Cambridge University Press 2014

First published 2014
4th printing 2016

Printed in Dubai by Oriental Press

A catalogue record for this publication is available from the British Library.

Library of Congress Cataloguing in Publication data
Shackleton, Caroline.
  Trapped! the Aron Ralston story / Caroline Shackleton and Nathan Paul Turner.
    pages cm. -- (Cambridge discovery interactive readers)
  ISBN 978-1-107-66998-7 (pbk. : alk. paper)
  1. Rock climbing accidents--Utah--Bluejohn Canyon--Juvenile literature. 2. Ralston, Aron--Juvenile literature. 3. Desert survival--Utah--Bluejohn Canyon--Juvenile literature. 4. English language--Textbooks for foreign speakers. 5. Readers (Elementary) I. Title.

GV199.42.U8S43 2013
613.6'909792--dc23

                         2013014268

ISBN 978-1-107-66998-7

Additional resources for this publication at www.cambridge.org

Layout services, art direction, book design, and photo research: Q2ABillSMITH GROUP
Editorial services: Hyphen S.A.
Audio production: CityVox, New York
Video production: Q2ABillSMITH GROUP

Contents

Before You Read:
Get Ready!

An amazing story of survival against all odds.

Complete the definitions with the correct words.

boulder

canyon

ledge

rope

gear

1 _____ : a long, strong line made of many pieces of material and often used for tying things or climbing

2 _____ : a large, round rock that has been made smooth by the weather

3 _____ : a flat shelf of rock

4 _____ : a deep valley with steep sides

5 _____ : equipment and clothes used for a particular activity

Words to Know

Read the paragraph and look at the picture. Then complete the definitions with the correct form of the highlighted words.

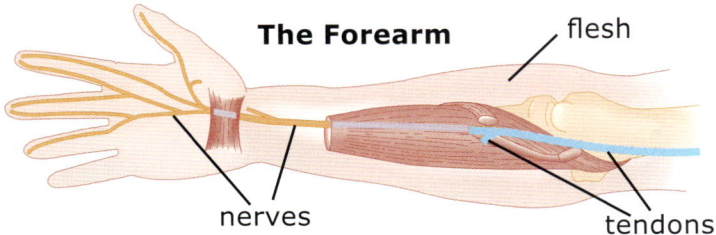

The Forearm

flesh

nerves

tendons

    Moving in and out of consciousness, Aron Ralston realized his arm would have to go. He would have to cut through the outer flesh, connecting tendons, and most painfully, the nerves of his forearm. First though, he would need to put on a tourniquet to stop his arm from bleeding.

1 _____ : the soft part of the body of a person or animal that covers the bones

2 _____ : the state of being awake and able to think

3 _____ : the thin, strong tissue that connects the muscle to the bone

4 _____ : the lower part of the arm between the wrist and the elbow

5 _____ : a piece of cloth that is tied tightly around an injured arm or leg to stop the flow of blood

6 _____ : the long, thin connectors that send messages to your brain

? PREDICT

What do you think Aron Ralston did to try to save himself before making the decision to cut his arm off? How long do you think it took him to realize he needed to cut his arm off?

CHAPTER 1

Day 1 – Trapped

WEARING SHORTS AND A T-SHIRT, WITH JUST A SMALL BACKPACK AND A LITER OF WATER, ARON RALSTON PREPARED TO CLIMB DOWN THE FINAL SECTION OF THE CANYON. . . .

He was now close to the bottom, just 150 meters from the end of the final climb. If all went well, he would soon reach the bottom, **hike** out to his truck 1.5 kilometers away, and drive back for the bike he had left behind at the top.

The space between the canyon walls measured no more than a meter across. He worked his way slowly down the canyon, pushing himself carefully between the narrow walls in search of handholds and supports. An experienced climber, 27-year-old Aron had already successfully climbed many of Colorado's highest peaks. In comparison, this climb was child's play. Aron hadn't even bothered to let anyone know where he was going, and had brought the minimum of necessary gear.

Concentrating on the task at hand,[1] he moved slowly but confidently down the canyon, only to find a large boulder blocking his path. To continue, he would have to climb up and over it. **Cautiously**, he climbed up onto the boulder, testing his weight. The boulder held firm. Aron moved carefully over the rock. Suddenly, just as he was moving past the other side, the rock came loose and fell towards him. Aron threw his arms out to protect his head as the rock came down. With a scream of pain, he felt the enormous boulder crash down on his right hand. Shaking from the pain and the shock, Aron slowly opened his eyes. What he saw filled him with horror. His right arm had been crushed[2] under the enormous, 360-kilogram boulder. He tried desperately to pull it out, but there was no way the rock was going to move. Aron was trapped.

[1] **at hand:** happening at this time
[2] **crush:** press down very hard on something so it breaks

?

EVALUATE

What could you criticize about Aron's preparation for his climb? What should Aron have done differently?

CHAPTER 2

Aron's Background

ALWAYS A RISK-TAKER, ARON RALSTON'S THIRST FOR ADVENTURE OFTEN GOT HIM INTO DANGEROUS SITUATIONS.

When Aron Ralston was 11, his family moved to Colorado. There, Aron fell in love with the Rocky Mountains, hiking and camping, and quickly learning to ski. When he was just 18, Aron and his best friend, Jon, climbed their first "fourteener," or 14,000-foot (about 4,200-meter) mountain.

During college, Aron worked as an outdoor guide. After graduating as an engineer, he climbed as much as possible. He would take risks and get into trouble, often when alone and in extreme weather conditions. When his job took him to New Mexico, he joined the local mountain rescue team, gaining valuable training from more experienced **mountaineers**.

In 2002, Aron quit his job as an engineer and moved back to Colorado – to Aspen, in the heart of the Rocky Mountains.

He got a job in a mountaineering store, and he continued to ski and climb, **conquering** over 30 of Colorado's 54 "fourteeners" alone and in winter.

Then, in February 2003, Aron and two friends were hit by an avalanche while on a cross-country skiing trip. They were almost killed. Aron had persuaded his friends to ski a very risky route down the mountain. Incredibly, none of them suffered serious injuries, but Aron's friends refused to speak to him again.

By now Aron had been involved in many accidents. Although he was experienced, his thirst for excitement constantly put him at risk, and he realized he needed to be more careful. Despite this, when Aron decided to drive almost 500 kilometers to Wayne County, Utah, for a simple climb down Blue John Canyon, he didn't mention his plans to anyone. Nobody knew where he was or what he was doing. On April 26, 2003, after spending the night in his truck, he cycled south to the canyon entrance. There, locking his bike to a tree, Aron set out on the hardest six days of his life.

Video Quest

Traverse Rock Climbing

Watch this video and find out how traverse climbing is different from traditional climbing.

CHAPTER 3

Days 1 to 4

TRAPPED IN BLUE JOHN CANYON, ARON TRIES DESPERATELY TO THINK HOW TO FREE HIS ARM.

At first, the pain had been so great that he could hardly think. He had panicked, screaming out then pushing and pulling desperately at the huge boulder to try and free his trapped wrist. Nothing! There was no way the rock would come loose. As the adrenaline[3] lessened, Aron was able to think more clearly about his situation. He knew he only had enough water to survive a few days or so at most. Unfortunately, however, the water bottle was in his backpack, and he wasn't sure he could get it out. Pulling his arm out of one **strap**, he pushed his head through the other one and managed to slide the pack down to his feet.

He drank from his water bottle so quickly that, before he realized it, almost a third of his water was gone. This was serious. He needed to save his water, or he would die for sure.

[3]**adrenaline:** a chemical produced by the body when a person is frightened, angry, or excited, which makes the heart beat faster and prepares the body to react to danger

He had to think seriously about his options. What were they? He looked at his things. Apart from his CD player and video camera, he had his water, his ropes and rock climbing gear, his cheap multi-tool knife, his camera, and a small flashlight. He could only think of two options. First, he could try to cut away the rock from around his arm, though this seemed impossible with the small knife he was carrying. Second, he could try to use his ropes to lift the boulder off his arm, but that also seemed impossible. Then suddenly he had a third idea that made him shake with fear. He could **amputate** his own arm. His hand was already turning gray through the loss of blood, and he knew that, if he didn't get free very soon, he would lose it. But cut off his own arm? "No," he thought, "anything but that."

A multi-tool knife

11

He decided to try to cut through the rock. After several hours, he had done little more than make a few scratches. Night had fallen and the canyon was turning cold. Exhausted and frightened, he sat back and tried to make himself as comfortable as possible for his first night in the canyon.

At dawn on the second day, he decided to try and use his climbing gear to lift the boulder off his arm. He had seen a rocky ledge above him, and he thought he might be able to throw his rope over the ledge and pull the boulder up. He spent two hours throwing his rope up until finally it caught. For the next few hours, he pulled on the rope with all his strength, but without success. The boulder didn't even move an inch.

Climbing ropes

For the first time, he began to think seriously about cutting off his arm. Aron realized he would need to tie something tightly around his arm to stop the bleeding. He decided to use a strap off his gear to make a tourniquet. He tied it tightly round his forearm, and then slowly moved his knife towards his wrist. He felt sick. He couldn't do it. He really couldn't. A wave of **despair** overcame him. He hated this place. He hated this canyon. He hated this boulder. Then, slowly, he calmed down. There was no one at fault here but himself. He should have let someone know where he

was going. As night came, he fell in and out of consciousness, losing track of time. And every time he woke, the terrible pain in his right arm reminded him of the hopeless situation he was in.

By day three he knew he had to amputate. He re-tightened the tourniquet and pushed his knife against the flesh above his wrist. It wouldn't cut. He couldn't believe it. It was so dull from cutting the rock the day before that it wouldn't even cut the skin. He had run out of options. Aron was desperate. Night came again. It brought more darkness, more cold, and more pain.

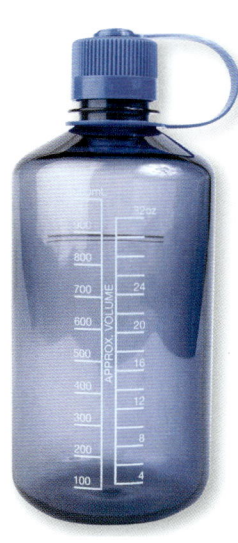

Water bottle

On the morning of day four, Aron felt close to the end. He had 90 milliliters of water left – just enough to fill a small glass. He knew there was little chance of rescue, and he began to accept the unthinkable: he was going to die right here in this canyon. He thought about his parents and his sister. He felt so stupid and guilty for the pain they would feel over his death. He got out his video camera and recorded a message for them. He told them he was sorry, how proud he was of them, and how much he loved them. Finally, he asked anybody who found his body to please make sure his parents got the video. When he finished, he felt strangely happy.

Suddenly, Aron remembered the shorter **blade** on his knife, which he had not used on the rock. Using all his courage, he pushed the blade hard into his wrist. Amazed, he looked at the blade stuck in his arm. He couldn't believe what he had just done. Surprisingly, there was no pain. It was as though his hand was already dead and no longer a part of him. He continued to cut with the knife until he felt it hit the bone. He tried, but there was just no way the little blade could cut through bone. He gave up, and in his despair he drank down the rest of his water. It felt so good.

Video Quest

The Colorado Plateau

Watch this video to find out about the Colorado Plateau area. What are its geographical and historical features?

CHAPTER 4

Days 5 and 6

ON THE FIFTH MORNING ARON AWOKE FROM HIS SEMI-CONSCIOUS NIGHTMARES KNOWING THAT HE NOW FACED CERTAIN DEATH.

He had tried everything. Unable to cut the rock away, he had ruined his knife in the process. The rope system he had invented to lift the boulder off his arm had had no effect at all. Finally, the horrible idea of cutting his own arm off had turned out to be unworkable. His small knife was totally useless against the hard bone of his arm.

Thinking back over the last five days, Aron calculated he had been trapped for 90 hours – most of them without sleep – and had been without water for almost 30 hours. He took out his video camera and spoke to his family one last time. Again, he told them he loved them, that he wanted them to be happy, that they should remember him with a smile.

The day was cool, and Aron knew that the next night would be the coldest yet. He knew he wouldn't survive, yet he was completely calm. He felt a disconnected sense of happiness, of freedom. He had accepted his situation.

As night came and the temperatures of the canyon fell to freezing and the wind screamed around him, Aron cut his name and date of birth into the rock. Below, he added the day's date, April 3, sure it would be the date of his death. He sat back and started to dream.

Among the pictures in his mind he saw a small boy, a boy he knew immediately was his son. He saw his son looking up at him, smiling. Then he saw himself, with only one hand, picking up the small boy, using his handless right arm to support him. They laughed together in the sunshine. Then suddenly, the boy disappeared. Aron was back in the canyon, still trapped in the cold night. But now, everything had changed. Now he believed, somehow, he would live.

By morning Aron had hardly any energy left. In sudden violent anger, he started to attack the boulder with a small rock, as if to break it into pieces. The rock sent horribly painful shocks up his left hand. He stopped, and cleared the pieces of rock off his trapped arm with his knife. By accident the knife cut his trapped hand. He didn't feel a thing as the knife sank straight in, letting out a terrible smell of gases. His hand was dead. All at once he hated it. He didn't want it, it was already dead and it was killing him, too.

He started to pull violently, screaming at his hand, hating it, trying to tear it off. Suddenly, with the violent movement of his body against the rock, he felt his arm bend.[4]

[4]**bend:** move something so that it is not straight

And then he understood: he could use the boulder. He could use the boulder to break the bones in his arm. Now everything had changed. Before, it was the boulder that was trapping him. Now he realized that it wasn't the boulder. His dead hand was trapping him. The boulder would set him free!

Without even thinking, hardly conscious of the pain shooting upwards into his arm, Aron sat back, pulling down with all his strength. He forced his arm down and to the left. Suddenly, with a loud crack,[5] one of the two bones below his elbow broke. For the other bone, he would have to push in the opposite direction. He used his feet to push himself up over the boulder. Despite the terrible pain, he threw himself forward again and again, feeling the bone bending. Finally, he heard the crack as it too broke.

[5]**crack:** a sudden short noise – the noise of something hard breaking

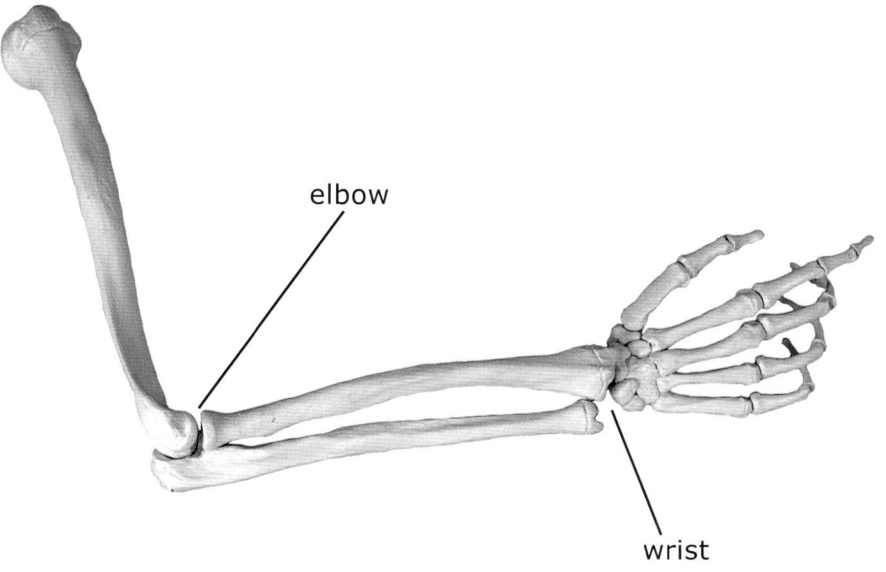

elbow

wrist

Pliers

That was it! He had done it. He could hardly believe it. Amazingly, the two bones had broken in the same place, and Aron knew he would now be able to cut off his hand. He tightened the tourniquet and used the smaller, sharper blade of his multi-tool to cut away the flesh of his arm. Finally, the only part left was also the most painful – the main nerves and tendons. He tried to cut the tendon, but the small knife did not help. He changed tools, using the pliers to bite through the tendon. Now there was only the nerve left. He placed the teeth of the pliers around the nerve, closed his eyes, and taking a deep breath, he pulled hard.

The pain was incredible, as if someone had set his arm on fire. He almost lost consciousness, and just for a few seconds his world went white. Then, as the pain faded, he opened his eyes. He was lying on the floor of the canyon, on his side. About a meter or so to his right he could see the boulder, and under it, the remains of his right hand. He was free!

He used his rope and straps from his gear to tie his right arm against his body and to stop the bleeding. He looked at the date of his death that he had cut into the rock only the night before. Then, forcing himself to look away from the hand he had to leave behind, he climbed as fast he could down to the bottom of the canyon.

CHAPTER 5

Life after Blue John Canyon

INCREDIBLY, ARON MANAGED TO WALK 10 KILOMETERS ALTHOUGH HE WAS WEAK AND BLEEDING HEAVILY.

Aron came across a family out walking for the day. Amazingly, they knew who he was. His truck had been found by the police, who had started a helicopter search of the area.

The family gave Aron water and cookies, and helped him to continue walking and stay conscious. He was getting weaker and weaker. Just when it seemed he could go no further, a police helicopter flew right in front of the group. The helicopter took Aron, still conscious and talking, to a local hospital where he was given treatment. Aron Ralston had survived.

Those six days in the canyon changed everything for Aron. He now had to live with one hand, learning again how to do little things like tie his shoelaces and write. But Aron soon returned to his outdoor life, using a special tool fastened to his right arm that allowed him to continue climbing.

His story quickly became well known around the world, and he

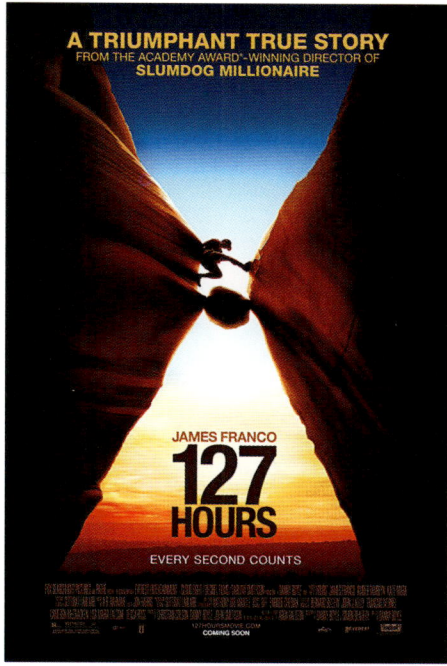

was asked to give interviews. His book about the terrible six-day ordeal[6] became a best-seller and was made into a successful Hollywood film. Aron became a star, and is a hero to many for his courage and will to live.

Most importantly, however, the events in Blue John Canyon changed Aron from a young, risk-taking adventurer into a responsible outdoorsman. Although he still has his love of adventure, he has learned to respect the dangers of nature.

What about the small boy in his life-saving dream back in Blue John Canyon? Well, in 2009, Aron married his girlfriend, Jessica, and in 2010 the couple had a baby boy. His name is Leo.

....
[6]**ordeal:** an experience that is very painful, difficult, or tiring

CHAPTER 6

What Would You Have Done?

1. Aron sets off without telling anybody his plans. He takes gear for one day, as the climb is easy and he'll be back tomorrow.

What should Aron have done? What would you have taken and why?

2. Halfway down the canyon, Aron's hand is trapped by a boulder. He thinks about the possibilities and realizes he can: a) try to break the boulder; b) try to lift the boulder; or c) amputate his own arm.

How would you have felt? Did Aron have any other options? What would you have done?

3. After spending his first night in the canyon, Aron tries to cut into the boulder. He is unsuccessful.

Would this have been your first choice? Why or why not?

4. Aron decides he can lift the boulder using his climbing ropes. He throws them over a ledge above, but cannot lift the heavy rock.

Do you think this could have worked? Should he have tried longer?

5. Aron realizes he must cut off his arm, but he cannot cut through the bones, and he stops.

Would you have been able to cut into your own arm? Describe your thoughts and feelings at this point.

6. Aron says his final goodbyes to his family. He cuts his name and the date of his death into the rock and waits for the end.

What would you have wanted to say to people? How would you have wanted to be remembered?

7. Aron dreams about his future son and starts to believe he will survive. He frees himself and walks 10 kilometers before being rescued by a helicopter.

What would have given you hope in this situation? How would you have kept going?

After You Read

Read the following sentences and choose Ⓐ, Ⓑ, Ⓒ, or Ⓓ.

1 Aron had made the mistake of _____ .

Ⓐ not telling anybody his location
Ⓑ not moving slowly enough
Ⓒ carrying too much equipment
Ⓓ climbing in a very difficult area

2 Aron's attempt to lift the boulder was unsuccessful because _____ .

Ⓐ he couldn't tie the ropes
Ⓑ the ropes were too weak
Ⓒ he couldn't reach the rock
Ⓓ the rock was too heavy

3 Aron was encouraged to keep going by a feeling that _____ .

Ⓐ his parents still needed his help
Ⓑ he had friends looking for him
Ⓒ he would have a child in the future
Ⓓ he would see his family again

4 In the end Aron managed to _____ .

Ⓐ walk back to the town
Ⓑ drive himself to a hospital
Ⓒ find people who could help him
Ⓓ get a ride with some mountaineers

5 After he recovered from his accident, Aron _____ .

Ⓐ started an outdoor climbing company
Ⓑ refused to go climbing again
Ⓒ went on to climb Mount Everest
Ⓓ had to re-learn many life skills

Complete the Sentences

Use the words in the box to complete the list of things to pack when going climbing.

| gear | knife | ropes | route | straps |

You need to pack the following **1** _____ in your backpack:

- Plenty of water – at least two liters per day. Attach the bottles securely to your pack with strong **2** _____ .

- A good quality **3** _____ or a multi-tool with a sharp blade, in case you need to cut something.

- Climbing **4** _____ , which should be in good condition. If they are old or worn, they may break.

- Recent maps. You should plan your **5** _____ before you leave using up-to-date maps of the area.

? ANALYZE

Organize the following events into the correct order and outline the events which led to Aron's escape.

A He gets angry.
B He ties his arm against his body.
C He uses his knife.
D He falls asleep.
E He uses his pliers.
F His bones break.

Answer Key

Words to Know, page 4

① rope ② boulder ③ ledge ④ canyon ⑤ gear

Words to Know, page 5

① flesh ② consciousness ③ tendons ④ forearm
⑤ tourniquet ⑥ nerves

Predict, page 5

Answers will vary.

Evaluate, page 7

Suggested Answer: He didn't tell anybody where he was going. He didn't take enough food, water, or clothing. He should have told people where he was going.

Video Quest, page 9

Suggested Answer: Traverse climbing is moving horizontally across the rock face as opposed to climbing up the rock face.

Video Quest, page 15

Suggested Answer: Mainly deserts, brightly colored rocks (some of which are natural monuments), and some forests. It has many streams that supply the water to the area. The rivers in the Great Basin do not flow into the sea. It has many national parks designed to protect wildlife. Native Indians have lived there for many years.

Choose the Correct Answers, page 26

① A ② D ③ C ④ C ⑤ D

Complete the Sentences, page 27

① gear ② straps ③ knife ④ ropes ⑤ route

Analyze, page 27

① D ② A ③ F ④ C ⑤ E ⑥ B